Come to the Water

The Psalms

by John Freal

2022

1i

Dedication –

    To my children and theirs

Cover art by Nicki Lang

Come to the Water – The Psalms

Library of Congress Control Number: 2021925714

ISBN: 9788985508901

Editor's Introduction

by Marla Tuski, counselor and spiritual director

If you love God, you are familiar with the movements of your heart and soul toward faith, hope, and love. You know the internal struggle between walking toward love, toward God, and running in another direction. I suggest that those most familiar with these movements love the Psalms.

If you pray the Psalms, you will appreciate how John has extracted the perfume infusing the psalmists' intimate and transparent expressions related to their movements of heart. John uses haiku and other prayer forms in his distillation process, resulting in prayer language that gets to the essence of our pain, our joy, our love, our longings. If you haven't prayed the Psalms, this work will be a lovely initiation.

The poems in this volume stir the heart toward love and devotion of our Lord, Creator, Rescuer, and Guide. There are many prayers here that can be used for one's own breath prayers – simple, memorable, profound that can be prayed through the day to open your heart to encounter God. If you endeavor to be shaped by the Holy Spirit, you will find this book to be a meaningful aid toward that end. There are words here that help you express a depth of sorrow, and others that help you let go of your anxious thoughts so that you can simply rest and wonder in God's presence. Other poems lead you to delight and exaltation. Read through slowly, stop and savor, let God meet you here.

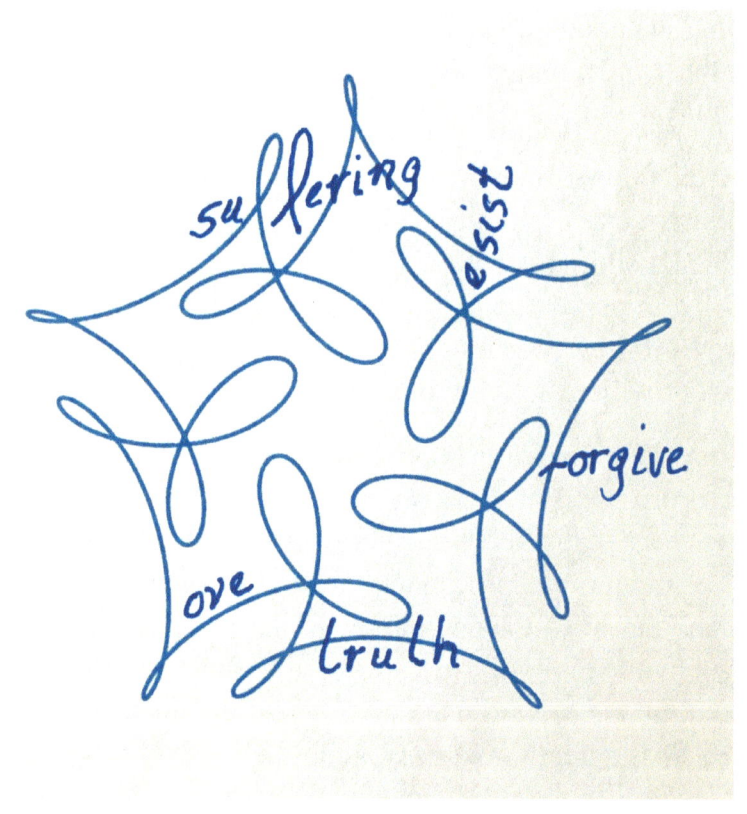

4i

Introduction

The crises we see in our world and in our personal lives are overwhelming. Though we can't even name them all, here is an attempt – falling into poverty or unemployment, personal or family discord, racism, sexism, homophobia, sanctioned and unsanctioned violence, ecological collapse, climate change, crumbling infrastructure, economic inequality, hostility to open societies, inadequate health care, streams of refugees, homelessness, lack of meaningful work, and the loss of social cohesion. All of these issues need the attention of some of us. Some crises need the attention of us all. Yet what I ask here is that you consider a crisis that is behind and beyond these other problems. This metacrisis is the loss of the sacred in our lives, our relationships, and our social imaginaries. Many have lost touch with sources of intrinsic value such as meaning, community, and transcendence. We need a spiritual awakening and a sense of the sacred in our lives and in the world at large.

Our culture needs religion, not religion as a particular set of beliefs but religion as a web of experiences. A secular culture devoid of religion probably can't pursue the common good. Neither can a religion which doesn't recognize the common good or truncates the spiritual to only beliefs and rules. Without a sense of the common good none of the crises mentioned can be overcome. We need a spiritual culture to replace violence with justice, fear with courage, and hubris with humility and whose goal is to build a larger life for all people.

Prayer will not be a substitute for the actions to which you are called along with others. It will, however, lead to better seeing. These psalms could work with *Lectio Divina* if that has been a way for you to enter into scripture. Since most of them are short, there's also the possibility for them to be rearranged as part of your own *Liturgy of the Hours,* matins, dawn prayer, mid-morning prayer, midday prayer, wisdom hour, vespers, and compline. I hope to do this sometime, but I haven't done it yet. I've prayed and lived with the Psalms for over 40 years and how I've used them has changed several times over those years. What I do mornings now is read a psalm or two or five and then enter a time of silence. That silence is punctuated by this prayer at the beginning –

Now no goal exists.
There's nothing here to achieve.
Love is who you are.

These three lines remind me of Thomas Merton's three-word instruction to novices, "Now…Here…This." This next prayer readies me for the day, reminding me of what I need most to do.

Seek and share presence.
Be thankful and grow forth to
plan, pray, and be kind.

These beginnings and endings use a Japanese form we know as haiku, a five syllable line, followed by a 7 syllable line, and ending with another 5 syllable line. Five years ago I wrote each psalm as a haiku and published the work as Poor Poet's Psalter. Some of those haiku are included here.

Haiku developed from renga, a form of collaborative poetry which began in 15th century Japan. The first stanza of a renga, called the hokku, was limited to 17 syllables. After one poet wrote the hokku, the next poet wrote a stanza with 14 syllables, and then the third stanza had 17 syllables again. The renga could continue like this for many stanzas, each limited in the number of syllables and required to connect to something in the stanza before it. The rules made the collaborative process fair and whole and also rather elaborate. Haiku as a stand alone developed as the collaborative gatherings of poets became less frequent. When I wanted to continue a haiku, I used the renga form though I had no one with whom I could collaborate.

Actually I have collaborated at a distance with three people. In 2002, Norman Fischer, a poet and Buddhist priest wrote a modern version of most of the psalms. His renderings were my prayers for several years. Several lines here have been stolen from him, some knowingly and probably some unknowingly. I met him in Bellingham where he was reading from his latest book of poetry in which most of the poems were even shorter than haiku. He signed a copy of my *Poor Poet's Psalter*.

Beginning in the 1990s I began to become acquainted with Eugene Peterson, not just through his books but also through his lectures and gatherings with friends in nearby Vancouver at Regent College. There are parts of scripture I can't read without hearing his voice.

My final collaborator is Robert Alter. His translation of the entire Hebrew Bible into English with extensive notes is a great gift to the world. Many of the psalms in this collection are a reworking of or inspired by his Hebrew versets.

Psalm 1 is a reworking of Robert Alter's translation of the Hebrew. Eugene Peterson called it a poem instead of a prayer. He characterized Psalm 1 as a pre-psalm, something that gets us ready to pray.

Beginning in Psalm 4 the Hebrew word that truly means rescue is sometimes translated as redeem/redemption or save/salvation. The words redeem and save tend to bring their own theological baggage by offering a present or future change for a past circumstance. The word rescue is used throughout the psalms to indicate an event happening only in the present. May these psalms be with you in your present.

Fault Lines – Psalms 1-41

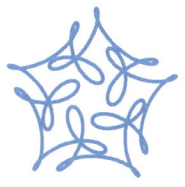

1

To be happy
   do not walk with the wicked
      nor stand with the twisted
         nor sit in the sessions of scoffers

God's teaching is written on your heart
   so you shall be like a tree by a stream
      that bears fruit in season
         and grows in root and branch

2

               We try to run from
            the kingdom of being to
              find another home

            Remember your creation
             You are a child of God

3

        My foes surround me
     but you bless me anyway
       I can live with that

4

       When I call to you
  and trust the truth of being
     I receive your light

   Whether asleep or awake
  you rescue and sustain me

5

Condemn them, O God
  Let them fall by their counsels
    Cast off their rebellions

So that all who shelter in you rejoice
  May they sing gladly in their prayers
    and in your presence find love

For you bless the just
  and listen well to their voices
    Like a shield you crown them with favor

6

Have mercy on us
for we are fading away
Only love saves us

7

Let the enemy
draw his sword and make ready
instruments of death

8

When I witness
  the wonder of the cosmos

I ask why you should care
  for any of us

Yet you have made us
  only a little less than gods

You remember us
  grounding us in love
    to rule over the work of your hands

9

You rebuke nations
and hear the cry of the poor
Seekers tell your deeds

I will tell of your wonders
because you granted me grace

10

Ambush and deceit
Lurking near the villages
Have you forgotten

Do justice for the orphan
Let these oppressors be gone

11

A shot in the dark
shakes our foundations until
You give us refuge

When the wicked bend the bow
what can the righteous ones do

12

Honesty is gone
Their language only makes lies
Your word keeps us whole

From those who plunder the poor
rescue us by your witness

13

How long will you forget me
  How long will you hide your face

Where shall I cast about for counsel
  Where shall I take the sorrow in my heart

How long shall my enemies laugh
  and exult when I stumble

For I trust in your kindness
  and look to the dawn of your rescue

This photo was taken at sunrise on Easter morning 2020. The stacks of stones were made during the night by persons unknown.

14

Fools cannot trust you
Only those with nothing left
Come to you in hope

We all can stumble at times
We surely will need rescue

15

Who dwells in your tent
Who speaks the truth in her heart
in hard times keeps faith

When she gives seeks no return
Takes no part in deception

16

I place my trust only in you
  You are my guardian
    the foundation of what is good

You are my portion and cup
  Your measuring lines bring delight
    and they mark a place of fullness

For you keep me in the light
  and you give me counsel
    My life rests in your presence

So my heart rejoices
  My spirit overflows with joy
    and my body finds peace

17

My heart opens as in a dream
  Listen well to my song
    Hearken to my guileless prayer

You have come upon me by night
  You have tried me and found no wrong
    Hide me in the shadow of your wings

On your pathways set firm my steps
  so my feet will not stumble
    so my fears will not take over

18

Enclosed by darkness
then rescued by your kindness
Cause our lights to shine

19

The heavens declare your glory
  and the night sky is the work
    of your hands
Day to day pours forth language
  Night to night flashes images
Their voice falls silent
  Yet the music plays everywhere
Its clear notes sound
  to the ends of the cosmos
The sun runs joyfully
  to the end of the heavens and back again
    with nothing hidden from its heat

Your patterns are beautiful
  reviving the spirit
Their eloquent truth makes all clear
  so that even I seem wise
Your ways are upright
  making the heart glad
    and lighting our path
Your love is pure and endures forever
  What you require is just
    It is what we truly need
It is more durable than gold
  and sweeter than honey

Who serves you is inspired
  and in following you finds reward
Who is free from error
  Yet you take hold of it and turn it right
Where there is confusion
  let me not become entangled
So I will be forgiven and able
  to continue to walk with you
May the words of my mouth
  and the meditations of my heart
be acceptable to you
  my rock and my rescue

20

We trust in your grace
Acting in your world may our
partials become whole

While some trust in chariots
we trust your nameless presence

21

Evil will not win
Steadfast love will keep us whole
You crown us with strength

22*

You abandoned us
Prisoners of the lie that
Work shall make us free

We call and hear no answer
and find no peace at night

Despised - rejected
Why have you abandoned us
empty in Dachau

The dogs circle around us
For our garments they cast lots

Life is suffering
You have been here all along
We live in your heart

We all go down to the dust
May your light be forever

22* *My rendition of this psalm is a meditation on suffering, reflecting on my father's role as a liberator of the Dachau concentration camp.*

23

You* are my shepherd
  I shall not want

You* lead me to rest in the sweet grasses
  and guide me by quiet waters

You* lead me on paths of justice
  and refresh my life

Though I walk in the vale of death's shadow
  you are with me so I fear no harm

Your rod and your staff
  show me each step

You prepare a table for me
  in the midst of my adversity

You moisten my head with oil
  My cup overflows

Let but goodness and kindness pursue me
  all the days of my life

And I shall dwell in your house
  for many long days

*The **you** on these lines speaks of God in the third person
changing to second person in "the vale of death's dark
shadow."

24

Maker of fullness
Who stands in your holy place
Who goes to the mount

You walk with the one who is
clean of hands and pure of heart

To Yahweh I lift my essence
  In you I trust
Let me not be shamed
  Teach me and rescue me
Daily my hope is in you
  Your kindness is forever
My immaturity temporary
  The crooked get straight
and the lowly get justice
  Your precepts are true
Blessed is your forgiveness
  Guide us past fear
Guide our children too
  Counsel us in your ways
Let my eyes be turned to you
  Grant me grace in my loneliness
Calm the distress of my heart
  From these dire straits deliver me
Watch my enemies and see my suffering
  Guard my life
and be my shelter
  Yahweh is our redemption

* This is an English translation of a Hebrew acrostic. There
is one line for each of the 22 letters of the Hebrew alphabet.

26

We are innocent
Your beauty is our wholeness
Test our hearts in fire

We recount all your wonders
singing out a thanksgiving

27

Your presence is hope
You are my light and rescue
Even in the dark

If I trust in your goodness
this singing will have no end

28

In you my heart trusts
Thanksgiving becomes my song
singing my delight

Rescue and bless your people
Tend them - always bear them up

29

Wind can break cedars
Your call shakes all foundations
Your voice blesses us

You make the wilderness shake
and give the people your peace

30

The pit of despair
held me until your morning
turned fear to dancing

You have undone my sackcloth
and covered my heart with joy

31

My life but a breath
I thought you had redeemed me
for in you I rest

I am worn out with worry
for my life is exhausted

I am a disgrace
to enemies and neighbors
even friends tease me

I've become a lost vessel
They speak harshly against me

You hear the pleading
of those who seek your shelter
You lift my spirit

At all times will I bless you
Your steadfast love gives me life

32

You teach us the way
If we are honest with you
forgiveness is ours

Deliverance surrounds us
and your counsel is our song

33

Not saved by armed might
Your presence provides defense
We trust your I Am

34

They cry out - you hear
You are close to the broken
bringing them home

Angels camp here and proclaim
Taste and see that God is good

35

Chaff before the wind
At my stumbling they gathered
evil for goodness

36

Do the wicked hearts
store up hatred for the just
scheming in the night

Justice will overtake them
In your light we shall find light

Like smoke they vanish
Oppressors of the lowly
when justice comes forth

In the heart your teaching lives
Your truth from aleph to tav

Delight in what is
and the rightness of your cause
will shine like the sun

Trust in what is and do good
Keep faith and walk with your God

Give up anger
Be quiet before what is
and wait patiently

You stumbled but did not fall
for I held you by the hand

I make your steps firm
and delight in your movement
Abide in my love

For I will bless your children
and rescue them from darkness

38

No health in my bones
My heart throbs and is broken
I ask for healing

Pain is always before me
Only you can be my help

39

Waiting silently
my heart grew hot within me
I spoke out rashly

What's the measure of my days
and is my lot as nothing

Mere breath is each one
They go about in shadow
not knowing their fate

From my failings you save me
for I place my hope in you

Harken to my cry
Don't make me the butt of fools
as I sojourn here

Let me catch my breath knowing
my departure will be soon

40

I waited patiently for you
  and you leaned forward
    and heard me

You raised me up from the pit
  from the mud and the clay

and set my foot upon a rock
  so that my step was firm

You put a new song on my lips
  and in my heart

That many may hear it
  and have confidence in you

Then I said - Here I am
  and my heart's desire became yours
    Your law the shape of my heart

May all that seeks you be glad
  and those who love your ways
    keep singing

41 *Betrayal and Repentance*

Perhaps we should have cared better for the poor
  Then we wouldn't see these evil days

We wanted to be guarded and kept alive
  and called to be happy in the land

We pleaded to you to grant us grace
  and heal us even though we offended

But one came to visit
  His heart spoke lies

Some nasty thing was lodged in him
  We hope he lies down and does not rise

The scoundrel left us in the lurch
  He ate our bread but was utterly devious

O God - give us back our innocence
  Sustain us as we stand before you

This ends Book 1

Blessed is our God
forever and forever
Amen and amen

Introduction - Book 2

This Book is subtitled Honesty and Trust because in the Psalms in general and in this Book in particular we find that we can speak honestly with God and develop our trust in God's presence.

I also wanted to comment on my own honesty and trustworthiness. In 2016 when I posted my haiku versions of all the Psalms, I began with this haiku title.

The Psalms in haiku

One each day as time permits

Aiming for essense

Then and in this revision (which has the benefit of Robert Alter's excellent translation and notes) I did aim for essense – mostly. Where the essense of a psalm or part of one went somewhere I couldn't pray, I didn't go there. I couldn't go for smoting enemies or other types of violence, glorifying the king, punishment or retribution, blessings for battle or military victory, and some of Hebrew history. In these cases I tried to find another theme in the psalm. The Psalms do contain violent passages, but even after 40 years of trying, I could not, can not pray there. Although I included this conscious editing in these psalms of haiku, renga, and Hebrew-like versets, I hope you will find a prayerful honesty that you can trust.

Honesty and Trust – Psalms 42-72

42

Why am I downcast
One day I will give you thanks
when wholeness is mine

My whole being thirsts for you
When shall I know your presence

My tears are my bread
They ask me – where is your God
I pour out my heart

Deep is calling out to deep
as your waves break over me

My hope is in you
for yet I will acclaim you
You will rescue me

By day you ordain kindness
By night your song is with me

43

Sighing I wander
Till your truth and light lead to
your holy mountain

It is you that will guide me
Send forth kindness and beauty

44

Scorn of our neighbors
Do not turn your face away
Shadow dark as death

We were sold for no great price
Yet we are still on your path

45

Not limits but you
We open to your wonder
standing anointed

Truth, humility, justice
will be our glory and crown

46

Be still and know me
I Am what humans hope for
Come – behold my works

47

Let our music play
forever in praise of you
ruler of the earth

48

All those great kings died
Really of little import
We know your kindness

Of justice your hands are full
Let the whole earth give you praise

49

Who trusts in their wealth
Riches will redeem no one
None lives forever

Yet will death have the last word
Will God's love come to an end

I Am called to us
God's light flashed for all to see
Hear the words of God

Your sacrifice does not satisfy
  nor the offerings you make
The life of the seas and the forests
  already belongs to me
All that lives in the fields
  lives and moves in me
Pay me instead your words of thanks
  Offer me your heart's intention
Call me so I can answer
  Even give me your sorrows
Do not recite statutes
  that you have not lived
Let your spirit speak to me
  in honesty and freedom

Turn your course and be a light
Find my kindness and rescue

51

Wipe away my crimes
Cleanse me from my transgressions
This evil is mine

Create for me a pure heart
Renew my spirit within

Your holy spirit
and the joy of your rescue
do not take from me

Let me sing to your presence
You won't spurn a broken heart

52

His mind devises disasters
  and he likes destructive words
He loves evil better than good
  a lie more than speaking justice
God is not his stronghold
  He trusts in wealth and power
God will surely sweep him up
  and tear him from his tent
But I will flourish like an olive tree
  I trust in the kindness of God

53

The scoundrel says in his heart
  There is no God
They are corrupt and commit crimes
  There is none who does good
All have turned away
  Not even one does good
May God restore our fortunes
  so that we rejoice again

54

Won't you take my cause
Foes have risen against me
They have sought my life

I know that you will help me
I offer my life to you

55

Friends betray – break trust
Knowing you will make me whole
Shelter from the storm

56
Enemies attack
I will praise you anyway
You collect my tears

Walking in the light of life
I know your lasting presence

Photo from Stations of the Cross at the Passion entrance of
the Basilica of the Holy Family in Barcelona

57

Take pity on us
Dawn is the hour of rescue
You save the oppressed

The skies hold your steadfast truth
Your kindness fills the heavens

58

Corruption comes in
The reward for the people
is to see it out

59

Lies they say to us
Let them be caught in their pride
You are the fortress

Though they prowl around like dogs
We shall sing of your kindness

60

Your people suffer
We wonder what can be next
Our defense – broken

You helped us in days of old
Through you we shall be strengthened

61

Shelter me from foes
On your mountain for all time
let me dwell with you

I call from the wilderness
Listen closely to my prayer

Quiet my spirit
You are my rock and rescue
I shall not stumble

My foes took pleasure in lies
Quietly their voices cursed

My hope is in you
I will trust you at all times
pouring out my heart

I am quiet only here
in your fortress of mercy

You are our shelter
Let all of us trust in you
We are but a breath

On the scales all together
we don't even weigh that much

Don't trust wealth or theft
or set your hearts upon them
God has said one thing –

I offer strength and kindness
being justice for all your deeds

63

I am wandering
in a dry and weary land
drinking in your strength

Your love is better than life
and I bless you while I live

64

Hope for all people
You guide the waters of life
Your bounty is ours

65

Now silence is praise
for to you all flesh shall come
Listener to prayer

You quiet the roaring seas
and the tumult of nations

66

The whole earth gives thanks
You brought us to a good place
through fire and ice

Though we were caught in a net
we found our freedom in you

67

We will praise the light
May your way be known to all
Be gracious to us

Let nations rejoice in song
The earth acclaim your rescue

68

Foes vanish like smoke
You give the lonely a home
Captives get freedom

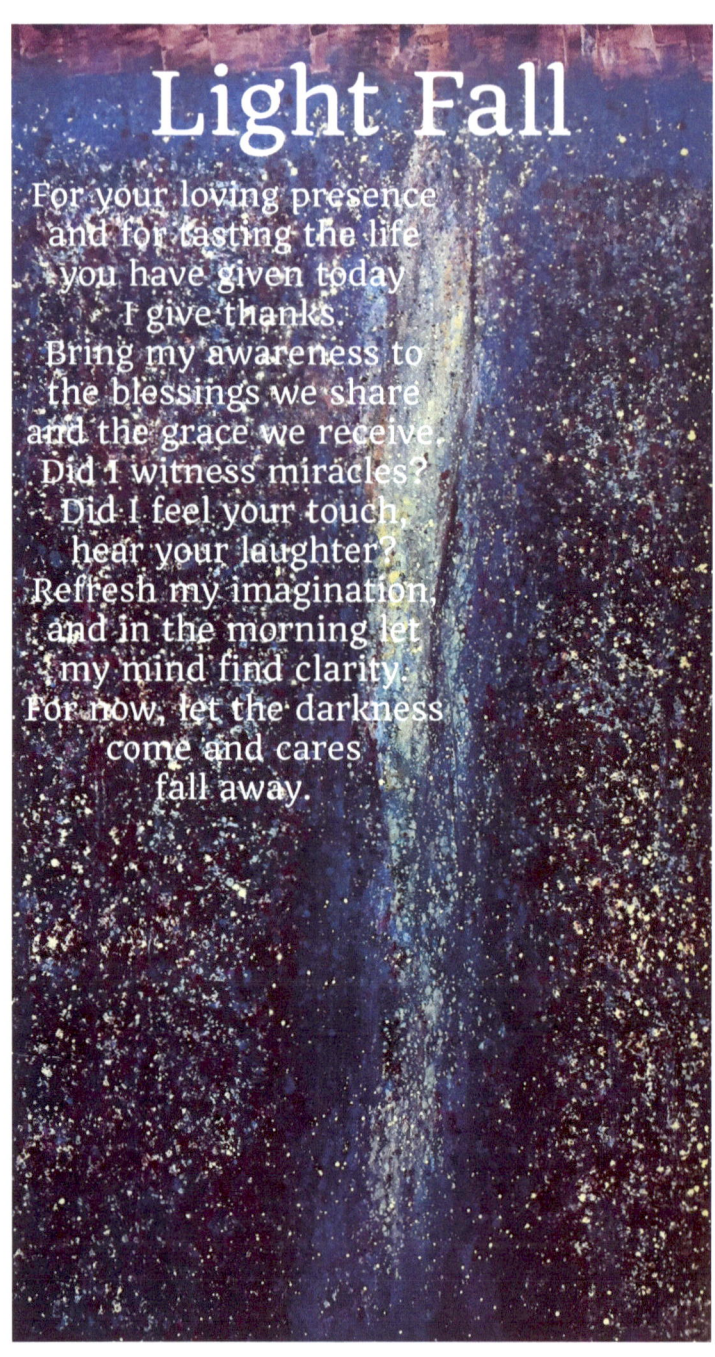

Light Fall

For your loving presence
and for tasting the life
you have given today
I give thanks.
Bring my awareness to
the blessings we share
and the grace we receive.
Did I witness miracles?
Did I feel your touch,
hear your laughter?
Refresh my imagination,
and in the morning let
my mind find clarity.
For now, let the darkness
come and cares
fall away.

There is no foothold
The waters have come up high
You know my folly

The current has taken me
Disgrace has covered my face

Reproach breaks my heart
I am lowly and hurting
Your rescue will save

You listen to the needy
Answer me with your kindness

God – deliver me
Let the shameful be confused
I need your help now

When my strength is spent
Rescue me from the unjust
You are my fortress

I've relied on you since birth
Be with me when I am old

When the poor call you
let the people see justice
like rain on the earth

Let the mountains and the hills
bear peace to all your people

End of Book 2

Amen and amen
For thus it has been written
and so I have heard

Running for Cover – Psalms 73-89

Though signs look hopeful, we may
need to spend a little more time in the
wilderness, time confined, time alone.
But not time wasted.

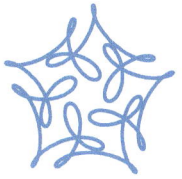

From John O'Donohue:

Awaken to the mystery of being here
and enter the quiet immensity of your own presence.

73

My feet almost strayed
I envied the revelers
for their healthy selves

They mock and speak with malice –
launch oppression from the heights

They pile up wealth
Do I turn to you in vain
Should I talk like them

Knowing what would be their end
I must be really foolish

Envy is no use
The arrogant meet their end
Swept out by terrors

You are the rock of my heart
and my portion forever

74

Have you cast us off
Give us reason to praise you
when these foes speak lies

Our own signs we did not see
Our prophet we did not hear

Worker of rescues
You shattered sea monsters
crushed Leviathan

Let the lowly praise your name
Yours is the day and the night

75

To the proud – let go
and to bullies – not so fast
Yahweh will be judge

I shall tell it forever
Let me sing always to God

76

War weapons broken
You inspire fear in the kings
Praise to you alone

So you rose up for judgment
to rescue all the lowly

77

Is our time ended
or will we see your power
a way through the sea

Blindly into the abyss
we proceed with your promise

78

You helped us often
and many times we complained
Help us be faithful

79

Holy place destroyed
Our dead not even buried
Rescue and forgive

We acclaim you forever
We are the flock that you tend

80

We have tears to drink
Our enemies laugh at us
Turn again – O God

Light up your face – rescue us
Restore us to life in you

Lift your voice in song
Blast the ram's horn at the moon
for God speaks these words

Since you called me in distress
I answered you in thunder

Do not give yourselves
to what becomes limiting
Just listen to me

I have opened your souls
and brought you to a clear place

Open wide your mouths
I will fill them with song –
unlimited song

But you do not hear so well
No willingness attends you

If you had heard me
the world would bend to the good
and time would be free

Listen for the harmony
and while you still may – sing out

God takes the stand in the assembly
  and in our midst renders judgment

How long will you judge dishonestly
  showing favor to the wicked
Bring justice to the poor and the orphan
  Vindicate the lowly and the different
Free the chained and the needy
  Save them from the oppressor's hand
You are children of the most high
  yet like all humans you shall die

83

Like chaff in the wind
As fire burns a forest
unless we seek you

84   *A Pilgrimage at Home*

You do not hold back
Happy the human who trusts
in walking with you

Early rains cloak your blessing
They make it into a spring

Highways of the heart
mark pilgrim journeys of those
who dwell in your house

Better is one day with you
than the wrong turns I have made

85

Undo your anger
Turn back – God of our rescue
Give us life again

We turn not back to folly
Let your grace dwell in the land

Show us your kindness
and grant rescue to us now
Peace and truth will meet

Truth will spring up from the earth
Kindness and justice will kiss

86

The insolent rise
unaware of your great love
Your servants trust you

Turn to me and grant me grace
and give strength to your servant

87
Happy those born here
May we be borne here again
Captured by your love

88

My cares are heavy
You've driven my friend away
Nothing more to lose

89

Will you always hide
As events crash over us
How long can we last

End of Book 3
Blessed be our God forever
Amen and amen

Open Hearts – Psalms 90-106

It takes courage to live with an open heart. However, that may be a tautology since an open heart is just courage seen from a different point of view.

From Luke 23/34

Father forgive them
They do not know what they do
or know you either

Help them wake up and grow up
free from their prison of lies

A burden to know
God inhabits all he creates
We can hate no more

Let us pray for our freedom
Let us find our souls in you

90   *A Psalm of Moses*

You have always been a refuge to me
  and to my ancestors
You are before the mountains and the seas
  before the cosmos from forever to forever
You turn me around
  saying return child
To you a thousand years are like yesterday
  like a lonely hour in the night
You rush them away like a flood
  like a long sleep – like grass
    that rises up fresh in the morning
      and by evening withers
All my days pass in your presence
  All my years reverberate
    like empyrean words

The years of our life number seventy
  Perhaps eighty if we are strong
Often then their span, their fullness
  is mostly toil and grief
Soon they are gone
  and we fly away
So teach us how to number our days
  that we may get a heart of wisdom

Satisfy me in the morning with your kindness
  and I will rejoice all day long
Show me how you live in me
  and give this blessing to my children
Light my path with your beauty
  and keep my life in your care
Let all that we do be yours
  and prosper the work of our hands

God of light rescues
Yahweh becomes a refuge
No fear of terrors

No evil rests in my soul
I will ride on eagle's wings

Your trust in the night
and kindness in the morning
are praise for what is

You created the cosmos
Its beauty is your making

Help me in growing
green like the basin cedars

From youth to old age
let me tell of your presence
in the company of light

93
Your goodness finds us
Beyond the thunder of waves
Past the end of time

Widow and stranger
are sacrificed by these fools
O God – be our help

Dig a pit for the wicked
You will not abandon us

Justice and judgment
will follow all the upright
The evil will fall

Sustain us with your kindness
and stand against injustice

*95 Who formed depths and heights
Help us listen to your voice
Let us sing to you*

96

Yahweh brings justice
Seas thunder and heavens sing
The whole earth is glad

God forms the world in justice
and peoples in faithfulness

97

Idols are worthless
The triumph of Yahweh is
joy for honest hearts

98

Nature rejoices
You come to judge the nations
and tribes with justice

Let the rivers clap their hands
and mountains sing together

99

Our heroes called out
You answered them from a cloud
forgiving their sins

Solving suffering is not
the way to live in wisdom

100

Our praise has a ground
– Your love endures forever –
faithfulness through time

Come to God in thanksgiving
God made us and we belong

101

Turn twisted hearts of
slander, arrogance, deceit
Help me find wisdom

Banish the speaker of lies
Let kindness and justice come

Give me a hearing
My days pass away like smoke
My heart is stricken

I forget to eat my bread
Sighing is my only voice

I'm just a shadow
seeing my life in the dust
marching to death's door

Yet on dust we take pity
and in ruins find beauty

You have not despised
the prayer of your lowly ones
We are as you see

We wear out like our clothing
in your presence all our years

Let my soul bless you
Let all my being bless you
Your gifts are gracious

You forgive our trespassing
and heal all our diseases

You redeem these lives
and crown us with compassion
abound in kindness

Not according to our wrongs
and our crimes do you treat us

For as the heavens
loom high over earth – so great
your loving kindness

As far as east is from west
so you have removed our sins

In forgiving us
you awaken the spirit
so lives are refreshed

Surely you know who we are
remember we are stardust

Our days are like grass
for we bloom and then are gone
The earth forgets us

and yet your kindness is from
forever to forever

May your creation –
all you made and are – bless you
I will bless you too

In all places – through all time
my soul is for your blessing

104

I will always bless your presence
  and see your signature in creation
From fire in the heavens
  to water on the earth
    you fashioned the cosmos
You cast seeds in space and time
  letting forces shape their dancing
May we listen to your gift of the earth
  and come awake with the world's greening
Let the rainbow remind us
  that your covenant is with all life

By the sea you watch orca swim and play
  chasing salmon for their food
You cover the mountains
  with forests of fir and hemlock
    and valleys with fields and cedars
You give us fruit and grain
  to gladden our hearts
The whole web of life is your gift
  Let birdsong remind us to be thankful
The earth is full of your riches
  Your deeds are done in wisdom

All creatures look to you for food
  and know the feeling of fullness
When you withdraw your breath
  they perish and return to the dust
When you send forth your spirit
  you renew the face of the earth
Let us sing to you while we live
  and always bless your presence

105

We sing praise to you
remember your faithfulness
opening the rock

Water flowed in the parched land
and we ate in the desert

106

We have been reckless
worshipping our golden calves
wounding our children

We forgot your kindnesses –
could not remember to pray

– End of Book 4 –
Amen and amen

Songs Along the Way – Psalms 107-150

Psalms 120 to 134 are known as the Psalms of Ascent, perhaps to be sung on pilgrimage to Jerusalem. The metaphor of a pilgrimage or journey can be a good context for praying the psalms through one's life.

107

We give thanks to you
  for you are goodness itself
    Your steadfast love endures forever
You rescued us from land and sea
  from east and west
    from north and south

Some wandered restless
  in wilderness and desert places
They could find no home with hunger
  and thirst their souls grew faint
In their straits they cried out to you
  and you delivered them to new homes

They could not help thanking you
  for your steadfast love
The rest of us heard as well
  Your goodness filled them
    and they had to sing

107 (continued)

Dwellers in death's dark shadows
  prisoners in iron shackles
They could not hear your counsel
  and grew deaf to your word
In their straits they cried out to you
  and you rescued them from darkness

They could not help thanking you
  for your steadfast love
The rest of us heard as well
  Your goodness filled them
    and they had to sing

Others were puffed up with their pride
  and wandered in a wasteland of lies
They could not eat the food you gave
  and choked instead on lies and death
In their straits they cried for you
  and you rescued them
    from their small selves

They could not help thanking you
  for your steadfast love
The rest of us heard as well
  Your goodness filled them
    and they had to pray

107 (continued)

Some go down to the sea in ships
  We do our work in the waters
We have seen many of your deeds
  and the wonders of the deep
Then you spoke and storms came
  The winds and waves
    took away our breath
We reeled and swayed like drunks
  and all our wisdom was swallowed up
We cried out to you in our poverty
  and you turned the storm to silence

We could not help thanking you
  for your steadfast love
The rest of them heard as well
  Your goodness filled us
    and we had to sing

108

Help against the foe
so that we may be rescued
and praise you again

109

They trade blame for love
My heart is pierced within me
My friends betray me

For they accuse me falsely
and return evil for good

110

You will be tested –
be refreshed along the way
Know God is with you

111

Holy is your name
and your presence brings justice
Praising you gives light

The beginning of wisdom is
awe that overflows my heart

112

Blessed by your presence
we can be generous and
a light in darkness

Happy are those who fear you
We keenly desire your word

113

Praise you forever
From the dust you raise the poor
to put them with kings

114

The sea rolls away
Israel comes from Egypt
Springs come from the rock

We wandered from ignorance
to find you with your people

115

To your name we give glory
  for your kindness and steadfast truth
Your invisible presence
  has created all that is

Their idols are silver and gold
  artifacts and ideologies
    merely human handiwork
A mouth they have but do not speak
  except to give false report
Eyes they have but do not see
  infecting their worshippers with blindness
Ears they have but do not hear
  and a nose that does not smell
Their hands do not feel
  Their feet do not walk
Their worshippers forget to think
  Their second-hand schemes
    will not satisfy
Those who make these idols
  and all who trust in them
    will be like them

O my people – trust only in God
  your help and your shield
God will bless you and your children
  and all who hear his voice
    and all who know her ways

116

I found sorrow when
cords of death encircled me
I called for mercy

I shall walk before God
in the land of the living

What can I give back
for all that I have received
for the gift of life

I lift the cup of rescue
and call on the name of God

117

Praise the Lord, all you nations
  Extol Him, all you tribes
For great is his steadfast love toward us
  and the faithfulness
    of the Lord endures forever
      Hallelujah

118

Give thanks to I Am
  for God is good
    Steadfast love endures forever
Let your clan say
    Steadfast love endures forever
Let your descendants always say
    Steadfast love endures forever
Let all who love I Am say
    Steadfast love endures forever

Out of my distress I called on you
  You answered and set me in a good place
    You have become my rescue
The stone that the builders rejected
  has become the cornerstone
This is the plan of I Am
  It is wondrous in our eyes

This is the day that I Am has made
  Let us exult and rejoice in it
Blessed is the one who comes
  who comes in the name of I Am
    bringing us light
Give thanks to I Am
  for God is good
    Steadfast love endures forever

119

Turn my heart to you
Open my eyes to your life
Your word is my light

120

Woe to this stranger
The path they seem to want is
war instead of peace

Save my life from lying lips
I called out and you answered

121

I lift my eyes to the mountains
  From where will my help come
My help is from you
  maker of heaven and earth
Who does not let my foot stumble
  My guardian does not slumber
With you there is no vagueness
  Nothing is murky or obscure
You are my guardian
  and you give me rest
The sun will not strike by day
  nor will the moon by night
You keep me from all harm
  and guard my life
You guard my going and coming
  now and forevermore

122

I rejoiced with those who said to me
  Let us go to your holy place
Suddenly our feet were standing
  within your gates
It is a place of unity
  where all tribes can gather

May we all gather here
  to pray for peace
For the sake of our companions
  let us pray and seek peace
For the sake of this place
  let us seek your goodness

To you I lift my eyes
 O God of the heavens
Humble and expectant do we all
 direct our gaze up to you
Let our spirits reflect your light
 and our hearts beat to your rhythms
Grant us grace now
 for we are sated with scorn
We feel the contempt of the callous
 and the disdain of the proud
We have had enough of false equivalence
 of willful ignorance and cultivated hubris
More than enough of fearful certainties
 of careless trumpery and private realities
  of ideological hysteria and junk religion

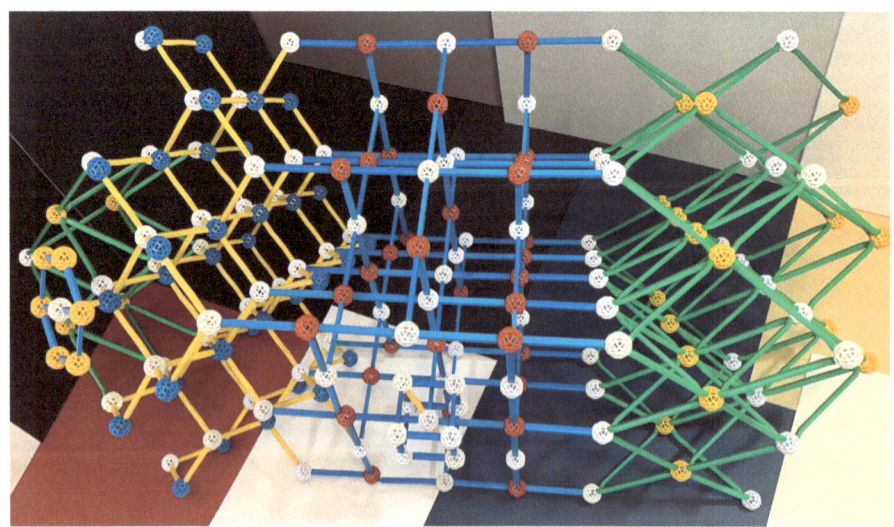

124

If you had not stood by us
  in our time of distress
If you had not stood by us
  we would have broken
When the floods came
  we would have been swept away
So we speak this blessing
  to you who have held us whole
To you who have kept us
  from all that is trapped, partial and torn
Because of you
  our souls flutter lightly
Like a bird escaped from a snare
  the snare is broken and we fly up

125

You encircle us
with paths leading to goodness
Not so the crooked

As mountains ring the city
shalom surrounds your people

126

We left in chaos
returned to our home singing
with a great harvest

Though we planted with our tears
we reaped with songs and laughter

127

Our children are gifts
Unless Yahweh builds with us
we labor in vain

128

Give us food to eat
Help us walk in your ways
families at peace

May we see our grandchildren
continue to grow in you

129

When we lose our way
we become our enemies
Our blessings wither

130

Forgiveness for us
Hope for all to find wholeness
My soul waits for you

More than watchers wait for dawn
we look for your steadfast love

131

I have settled down
finding calm and contentment
pride gone from my heart

I do not strive for greatness
Find trusting you is enough

132

We won't return home
can't even rest till we find
the place where you are

133

We look to being
together in unity
your blessing for us

134

At night we bless you
in holy places find you
lifting up our hands

135

Perhaps it will be
that they become like other
gods they have worshipped

Idols of the rich and proud
have a limited being

All that you desired
in the heavens and on earth
at sea and on land

We witness sun, clouds and rain
a rainbow for your promise

136

You give us kindness
The cosmos is your wisdom
Your love never dies

The earth is full of your glory
Steadfast love is forever

137

I sat down and wept
in this strange land of exile
I remembered home

Thoughts of vengeful violence
cross my mind and rend my heart

138

I walk through troubles
and remember to give thanks
Your hand preserves me

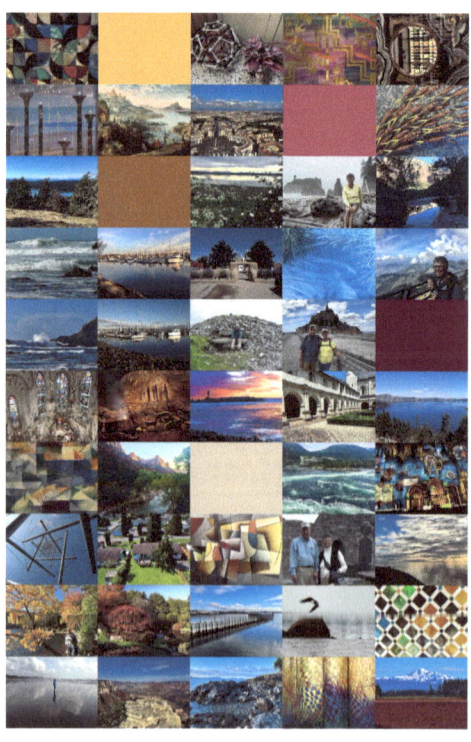

139

You searched me and you know
  You know my sitting and my rising
    and fathom my thoughts from afar
My path and my lair you assess
  and with all my ways are familiar
You think my thoughts before I do
  From behind and in front you shaped me

Where can I go from your spirit
  If I soar in the heavens
    you are there
Whether I fly with the dawn
  or dwell by the sea
    your hand leads me
Darkness cannot cloak me
  the night will glow like the day
    Darkness and light will be one

My frame is not hidden from you
  when I was made in secret
    knitted in the depths of time
My days are written in you book
  each with your presence
Your thoughts are more than the sands
  more beautiful than the dawn
Search me and know my heart
  Probe me and know my mind
Lead me away from selfishness
  to the way without end

140

Free us from evil
Protect us from violence
Rescue your people

The poor dwell in your presence
and you will take up their cause

141

I just might be wrong
Let the honest correct me
My heart turns to you

142

No refuge remains
There is no one who knows me
No escape exists

You will save me from darkness
You are my lot and shelter

143

O God – hear my prayer
  in your faithfulness answer me
For the enemy pursued me
  and made me dwell in darkness
I stretched out my hands to you
  my very self in need of rain
Do not hide your face
  lest I be like those gone down
In the morning let me hear your kindness
  for in you I trust
To you I lift up my being
  Let me know the way I should go
Teach me to follow your will
  for you are my God
On level ground
  let your spirit guide me
Keep giving me life
  for I am your servant

144

We are but a breath
and our days like a shadow
Yet your blessings come

May our hearts bless you
Of your grace and steadfast love
our children will know

Every day let me bless you
Bless your name forever

The next psalm *145 was first written by a pastor in 1869.
Not all the verses here are his.

*145 *How Can I Keep from Singing*

Through all the tumult and the strife
  I hear its music ringing.
It sounds an echo in my soul.
  How can I keep from singing?

While though the tempest loudly roars,
  I hear the truth; it liveth;
And though the darkness 'round me close,
  Songs in the night it giveth.

No storm can shake my inmost calm
  While to the Christ I'm clinging.
Since love is lord of heaven and earth,
  How can I keep from singing?

I lift my eyes; the clouds grow thin.
 I see the blue above it,
And day by day the pathway thins
 Since first I learned to love it.

The peace of Christ make fresh my heart,
 A fountain ever springing.
All things are mine since I am God's
 How can I keep from singing?

I see my neighbors and their loads;
 To share it is our calling.
Christ is our rescue and our hope,
 In grace when we are falling.

The spirit's gifts are for our friends
 Since love to share we're bringing.
God's kingdom lives in love we share.
 How can we keep from singing?

146

Praise God – O my soul
  Let me praise while I live
Do not trust in a human
  who offers no rescue
When our breath departs
  our palns become naught
Maker of heaven and earth, the sea
  and all that is in them
    you keep faith forever
You bring justice for the oppressed
  give bread to the hungry
    and freedom to captives
You give sight to the blind
  guarding the path of sojourners
    Your dominion is forever

147

You care for Zion
and heal the broken-hearted
Put songs in our hearts

Call out to Yahweh with thanks
and exalt in God's presence

148

Praise God from the heavens
  Praise Yahweh from the heights
Give praise – you messengers
  Sing anthems – you angels
Praise I Am – sun and moon
  and all you stars of light
Praise your creator
  particles of the cosmos
Let all beings on earth
  Give praise and thanks
Praise from the sea and the wind
  from fire and rain
Mountains and hills
  fruit trees and cedars
Wild beasts and domestic animals
  crawling things and winged birds
Leaders of the earth and nations
  young people and elders
Let us all praise I Am
  and exalt in this presence
    O Hallelujah

149

God loves all people
gives justice to the lowly
who sing a new song

To Yahweh we keep singing
Victory – Hallelujah

150

Praise God with a hunting horn's blast
  Praise with your hands on a harp
Praise I Am with dance
  even with banging pots and pans
Let all that has breath
  praise Yahweh – Hallelujah

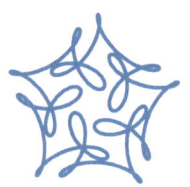

Open to Sorrow

No one escapes suffering
Pain makes a sound
and the whole world is humming
The losses accumulate
as we're called back
to acknowledge what happened
to honor these losses
and to what we can't make right

Do not harden your heart
Grief deepens compassion
It is part of the dance
(and sometimes seems like the whole of it)
this slow emptying of our days

So welcome the grief
whatever its form
Be generous to every sorrow
everywhere
Open your heart
Our sorrow connects us
No kindness is wasted
nor is compassion empty
This work is God's calling

Welcome by Thomas Keating

Welcome
Welcome
Welcome

I welcome everything   that comes to me today
                            for I know it is for my healing
                                                    growing
                                                    being

            I welcome all thoughts
                           feelings
                           emotions
                           persons
                           situations
                           conditions

                        for   power
                                control
I let go of my desire   for   affection
                                esteem
                                approval
                                pleasure
                        for   survival
                                security
                        to change any situation
                                        condition
                                        person or myself

        I open to Your   Love
                              Presence
                           action within
                           healing and grace

            Amen

A Prayer for Beginning

Joy flows from jazz riffs
We have much to contemplate
Art carves a pathway

Liturgy of beginning
Guide this impulse of making

Receive a vision
No forcing or holding back
What never has been

Open to play and learning
Open to service in Christ

For us / with us / within us

Who Are We?

We're all these
lovely contradictions
found in our truths
as well as our fictions
so let compassion
be the art
to open our minds
and open the heart
accept these selves
these forms and moods
forgive the clumsy attitudes
begin to see
our God in others
seeking communion
with sisters and brothers

A Loss to the Tigers

After stalking the wanderers to the edge of the forest
the three big cats attacked the weakest
the young and the old
expecting the rest to scatter and run
But the prey all fought for each other's survival
one of the cats was bruised
and for a while licked her wound
at the edge of the fray
In the end for their own protection
the cats had to kill them all
more than they wanted to kill
more than they could eat that week

An age later
scientists found the gnawed bones
of the 17 humans who fought for each other
who danced each other's rhythms
and found them beautiful

Coming Back to Church

With grateful hearts we return
though we come by way of grief and sorrow
hoping to end our laments
wanting to walk with you
What to clear away
to uncover your vision
of justice and peace
What way in the wilderness
to the rivers running in the desert

You created us one
You created a multitude

I went to the mountains
There I saw one standing
at the edge of the road
like Mary Magdalene
her feet in snow
her hands folded in prayer
her face turned toward a dying tree
I join my prayer with hers
Turn our fears to dancing
Set the shattered free
and break every yoke

You created us one
You created a multitude

I went to the sea
– You bade us come to the water –
and felt the chill of the gale
and stood by the sea stacks
called Shark's Teeth
There I waited for your children
They came
and we heard your voice in the wind
You wrote on our hearts
You write on all hearts
no matter who we are
no matter who we love

You created us one
You created a multitude

We are here to witness the light
the light of dawn
the light that Mary saw
in the garden / in angels / in Jesus
the resurrection light
the light of Christ
the light of the world
the light that shall be for all people
the light that shines in the darkness
the light that gives life
the Spirit that gives life
the light that turns to love
the love that overcomes
suffering and death and darkness

You create us today
– one and a multitude

Photo Sources - taken by the author unless stated otherwise

Lone heron in Drayton Harbor (title page)
Complex wave form with 5-fold symmetry (4i)
Crater Lake (3)
Oregon coast just south of Newport (4)
Semiahmoo Bay from Blaine Marine Park (7)
Drayton Harbor reflecting, twice (9)
Reflection of my wife Mel at the beach (11)
Looking toward Deception Pass from Mt. Erie (12)
Japanese Garden in the University of Washington
        Arboretum (15)
Frosty windshield (21)
Looking north from Mt. Erie (28)
A rose captured by Virginia Hennessy Freal (30)
Passion entrance of the Sagrada Familia in Barcelona (34)
Beach at Westport WA (36)
Portion of a work by Matsumi Kanemitsu (40)
Woodpile near Blaine (42)
Good Friday candles during the pandemic (48)
Looking toward Mt. Baker across Drayton Harbor (51)
Cairo tessellation on a sidewalk in Bellingham (52)
Ridge in fog near Fairbanks by Brian Lotze (54)
Eagle launching in Drayton Harbor (56)
Waves on the Oregon coast (57)
Grand Canyon (58)
Winter blueberry bushes and Mt. Baker (65)
Homeomeric tiling collage using advertising cards from art
        galleries in Santa Fe (75)
Looking west from the west shore of San Juan Island (77)
Transformations of 3 apeirohedra (78)
Flock in flight - Drayton Harbor (79)
Collage of 50 rectangular photos (84)

www.ingramcontent.com/pod-product-compliance
Lightning Source LLC
Chambersburg PA
CBHW040903120626
46551CB00006B/631